Gaylord Nelson

Other Badger Biographies

Gaylord Nelson

Champion for Our Earth

Sheila Terman Cohen

Wisconsin Historical Society Press

Published by the Wisconsin Historical Society Press
Publishers since 1855

© 2010 by State Historical Society of Wisconsin

For permission to reuse material from *Gaylord Nelson: Champion for Our Earth* (ISBN 978-0-87020-443-2), please access www.copyright.com or contact the Copyright Clearance Center, Inc. (CCC), 222 Rosewood Drive, Danvers, MA 01923, 978-750-8400. CCC is a not-for-profit organization that provides licenses and registration for a variety of users.

wisconsin**history**.org

Photographs identified with WHi or WHS are from the Society's collections; address requests to reproduce these photos to the Visual Materials Archivist at the Wisconsin Historical Society, 816 State Street, Madison, WI 53706.

Printed in Wisconsin, U.S.A.
Designed by Jill Bremigan

14 13 12 11 10   1 2 3 4 5

Library of Congress Cataloging-in-Publication Data
Cohen, Sheila, 1939-
 Gaylord Nelson : champion for our Earth / Sheila Terman Cohen.
 p. cm. — (Badger biographies)
Includes bibliographical references and index.
ISBN 978-0-87020-443-2 (pbk. : alk. paper) 1. Nelson, Gaylord, 1916–2005—Juvenile literature. 2. Legislators—United States—Biography—Juvenile literature. 3. United States. Congress. Senate—Biography—Juvenile literature. 4. Environmentalists—United States—Biography—Juvenile literature. 5. Conservationists—United States—Biography—Juvenile literature. 6. Earth Day—History—Juvenile literature. 7. Environmental protection—United States—History—20th century—Juvenile literature. 8. United States—Environmental conditions—Juvenile literature. 9. Governors—Wisconsin—Biography—Juvenile literature. I. Title.
E748.N43C64 2009
328.73092—dc22
[B]
                    2009026496

Front cover: Courtesy of Tia Nelson. Back cover: WHi Image ID 47078.

∞ The paper used in this publication meets the minimum requirements of the American National Standard for Information Sciences—Permanence of Paper for Printed Library Materials, ANSI Z39.48-1992.

Dedicated to my grandsons, Gabriel, Isaac, and Zev,
who are learning to be very good keepers of the Earth

Publication was made possible, in part, by gifts from Mrs. Harvey E. Vick of Milwaukee, Wisconsin, and from the friends of Ellen Nicolaus Purcell, in her honor. Additional funding was provided by a grant from the Amy Louise Hunter fellowship fund.

Contents

1

A Man Who Stood Up for His Beliefs

Have you ever believed in something that wasn't popular? Maybe your friends thought that your idea wasn't cool. You may have thought that you could not accomplish very much alone. If so, you probably know how hard it was to stick to your belief. It might have felt easiest to just go along with the crowd. Gaylord Nelson, one of Wisconsin's greatest leaders, knew those feelings, too. But he also learned that one person's ideas, words, and actions can change things for the better.

In the 1960s, few people understood that their daily lives were affecting the **environment**. They didn't realize that each time they threw a soda can on the ground or sent out gasoline fumes from their cars, they were adding to the problem of **pollution**. Gaylord Nelson saw that such careless actions were spoiling our air, water, and forests. He knew that something had to be done. So, he decided that he must lead the way in

environment (en **vi** ruhn muhnt): the natural world of land, sea, and air in which people, animals, and plants live
pollution (puh **loo** shuhn): something that dirties or destroys the natural environment

helping people understand how important it is to protect the land and all of its **natural resources**.

It took him many years, many attempts, and some failures before he was able to convince others that the gifts of our environment were in trouble. "The **crisis** of our environment is the big challenge facing mankind," he warned. Sometimes he found it very hard to stand alone. But Gaylord Nelson believed that each person could do something. So, he kept speaking out and working hard until people began to listen.

In his roles as a state **senator** and governor of Wisconsin, he supported laws that **preserved** some of the most beautiful and untouched lands in the state. Today, those lands are there for people to enjoy as they picnic in parks or hike miles of trails. Later, as a United States senator, he promoted laws that provided cleaner air and water. He also founded **Earth Day**, to honor our planet and to help people find new actions to protect it.

Chances are you and others in your school have helped Gaylord Nelson change the world—even if you didn't know

natural resource: a material that is part of nature, such as water, air, and plants   **crisis** (krɪ sis): a time of danger and difficulty, or a turning point   **senator**: a member of the Senate, which is one house of state or federal legislature   **preserved**: protected something so that it stayed in its original state   **Earth Day**: a day first set aside on April 22, 1970, to call attention to the environment

it. You may have done so by cleaning your school grounds or picking up garbage that was tossed in your favorite park. Maybe you made sure you put your used soda can in a recycling bin. Some of you may have planted a tiny tree in the woods or scattered flower seeds along a roadside. Maybe you did these things on your own. Or maybe you joined with others as part of an Earth Day celebration.

On Earth Day, citizens march near the Wisconsin state capitol.

Earth Day was Gaylord Nelson's idea. He thought, Why not set aside a special day to help people remember that each of us on this planet must take care of our natural resources if we want to continue to enjoy our surroundings? Why not teach people how to care for our natural world? His idea became reality on April 22, 1970, when the first Earth Day took place.

3

Since then, people throughout the country have participated in Earth Day activities. Eventually, the idea stretched from the United States to nations all over the world. In 1990, 140 countries took part in Earth Day events. Since then, Earth Day has brought together more than one billion people for activities to help the environment. Earth Day has become the largest nonreligious event in the world.

Gaylord Nelson strongly believed that each individual could do something to make our Earth a cleaner, safer, and more beautiful place to live. Earth Day seemed to be the spark that caused his belief to spread. **Legislators** began to make laws that would help to protect our environment. People in big cities and small towns began to realize that they needed to do their share, too.

Gaylord Nelson's story is an example of how each of us can do something to improve our own lives and the lives of others. By turning his ideas into actions, he had a powerful effect. He made the world a better place.

legislator (**lej** uh slay tur): someone who writes and passes laws

2

The Seeds of Good Ideas

Gaylord's childhood home still stands in Clear Lake, Wisconsin.

MARCUS COHEN

Just the way plants begin as seeds, so, too, do ideas. Ideas also must be nourished by their surroundings in order to grow strong enough to become actions. The seeds of Gaylord Nelson's beliefs were planted when he was a very young boy. His family and others whom he admired played a large part in nourishing his ideas. His childhood hometown of Clear Lake, in northwestern Wisconsin, was a fertile place for those ideas to **flourish**.

flourish (**flur** ish): grow and succeed

5

PHOTO COURTESY OF TIA NELSON

Gaylord as a young child

Gaylord came into the world on June 4, 1916, surrounded by a very busy household. His oldest sister, Janet, was just 3 years old. His sister Peg had not yet reached her second birthday. The Nelson household was filled with the voices of 3 little children. A couple of years later, on the very day that Gaylord turned 2, his younger brother, Stannard, came along. Whether they liked it or not, the 2 brothers had to share their birthday party each year. Chances are, Gaylord didn't grumble too much; he was a pretty **easygoing** kid. In fact, when an older boy in his neighborhood teased him by calling him "Happy," the name stuck. It suited him so well that just about everyone who crossed paths with Gaylord during his school years knew him as Happy Nelson.

The Nelson home always seemed to bustle with activity. The high-spirited sounds of children playing often mixed

easygoing: relaxed

6

with the voices of townspeople who would stop by to visit Gaylord's parents. Even complete strangers would drop in. Everyone in town knew that they would be welcomed at the Nelson household for a chat, a meal, or a place to stay.

When Gaylord was born, only about 700 people lived in Clear Lake. It was such a friendly place that

Clear Lake had a population of about 700 when Gaylord was growing up.

very few people ever bothered to lock their doors. When you walked down the street, most people would know who you were. Certainly Gaylord's family was well known and well respected in the town. His father, Anton, was the doctor for many families, and his mother, Mary, was a nurse.

The office of Anton Nelson, the Clear Lake doctor

His parents' work planted an important seed in Gaylord's life from the very start. Both of them were always busy helping their community. Aside from being a family doctor, Anton was the president of Clear Lake Bank. Mary was the head of the **Red Cross**. She was also very active in the **women's suffrage** movement that fought for women's right to vote. August 26, 1920, was a big day for Mary. That was when the United States passed a law that allowed women to become active participants in the voting process.

Red Cross: a worldwide organization that helps victims of disasters such as earthquakes, floods, and war
women's suffrage (wim uhnz **suhf** rij): the right for women to vote in elections, earned in 1920

Women's Suffrage Movement

Gaylord's earliest exposure to **politics** came from his parents' concern for **equal rights**. The Nelson family worked to make sure everyone in the U. S. was treated the same. His mother's leadership in the women's suffrage movement was a good example of that work. Although some countries throughout the world already allowed women to vote, the United States lagged behind. In the early 1900s, groups of women and men joined together in marches and speeches to speak out against the denial of such a basic right to women. The movement caught national attention. In 1920, President Woodrow Wilson

WHI IMAGE ID 5157

Mary Nelson was very active in the women's suffrage movement, like the women shown here.

proposed that it should be illegal for federal or state governments to deny a citizen the right to vote just for being a woman. That idea eventually became the nineteenth amendment to the United States Constitution.

politics: the way a city, state, or nation governs itself   **equal rights**: the same rights given to all people, regardless of their race, gender, or age

When Gaylord was growing up, doctors of that time would visit sick patients in their homes. Sometimes when Gaylord's father would make house calls, Gaylord would beg to go along. It was a treat to crank up their Model T Ford and climb in for a ride. But the automobile was still so new that many small towns lacked snowplows. On some winter days, the roads were piled high with snow. Then, Dr. Nelson and Gaylord would hitch up the family horse to a sleigh and off they would go. For a time, Gaylord thought that he might want to be a doctor and help people just like his father.

When snow was heavy, Dr. Nelson would visit patients in a horse-drawn sleigh like the one shown here.

WHI IMAGE ID 32635

WHI IMAGE ID 56636

The Nelson family owned a Model T Ford like this one.

Clear Lake was a place of great natural beauty.

Another seed that was planted early in Gaylord's life was his great love of the outdoors. The town of Clear Lake had a small city center that was surrounded by many acres of forest and several lakes. Gaylord never tired of poking around in the woods for creatures that were hiding under every leaf and rock. On long summer days he might sling his fishing rod over his shoulder and walk down to the shore of Clear Lake. He would step barefooted into the cold water to wait for the fish he would catch for dinner. When the same lake froze in the winter, he and his friends would put on skates and glide across the solid ice for hours at a time.

Gaylord often thought that the things he learned and did outdoors seemed much more interesting than the lessons

11

he was supposed to learn inside his classroom. For example, at the same time every spring, as sure as the sun rose in the morning and set at night, he saw the turtles crawling across the

WHI IMAGE ID 5898

same street in town. The slow-moving turtles would creep from Clear Lake to Mud Lake to lay their eggs. One day, Gaylord and his closest boyhood friend, Sherman Benson, decided to try an experiment.

Gaylord and his good pal Sherman Benson

The 2 boys wanted to see if they could trick the turtles into taking another route. When they saw the group plodding slowly across the street, the boys picked up a few turtles and turned them backward. Gaylord and Sherman turned other turtles sideways. They even carried some of the turtles away from the large group. To the boys' surprise, the turtles' natural **instincts** outsmarted their own human curiosity. Before they knew it, the turtles were lined up again, slowly, steadily moving toward Mud Lake.

instinct: behavior that is natural rather than learned

Gaylord and Sherman never did figure out how the turtles got to be so smart!

Once in a while, Gaylord's sense of humor and curiosity sprouted into a bit of mischief. When they were little boys, Gaylord was faster at math than his brother Stannard. After all, Gaylord was 2 years older. One summer day at a Clear Lake picnic, a nice neighbor gave Gaylord a nickel. Stannard was given a dime. At that time, Gaylord's nickel would buy a single-scoop ice cream cone. He knew that Stannard's dime would buy a double scoop.

Gaylord put his nickel next to his brother's dime. I'll trade you, he said. Stannard stared at the 2 coins. He could see that the nickel was larger. Gaylord convinced his brother that the bigger coin would buy more ice cream. Stannard happily made the exchange. But Gaylord always felt guilty for tricking his brother in

Gaylord with his younger brother, Stannard

that way. Much later in life, he sent Stannard a $500 check for the "loan," plus the cost of "criminal **penalties.**"

Gaylord and his friends were always up to something. One day they decided that Mr. Linderson, a banker who lived across the street from the Nelsons, might need a little humor in his life. So the boys made a plan. They staked out a place where they could easily see the Lindersons coming and going. Just as soon as they saw that the banker and his family were out of the house, they ran to get a small **heifer** that one of the boys owned.

The boys walked the cow down the street to the Lindersons' house and placed it right in the middle of their living room. You can imagine the family's surprise when they returned to find 2 big brown eyes staring at them! Gaylord was never sure how the joke was received, but he and his friends hooted with laughter from across the street.

Later, one of Gaylord's neighbors said that "they were more apt to help you than hurt you," even though the boys pulled a lot of pranks.

penalty (**pen** uhl tee): punishment   **heifer** (**hef** ur): a young cow that has never had a calf

Gaylord's young life was not always full of fun. When he was 10 years old, he came home one day feeling very sick. His head felt as if it was on fire, and he ached all over. Gaylord had come down with **rheumatic** fever.

At that time, rheumatic fever was a very frightening disease that was often deadly to children. Medications that would cure rheumatic fever had not yet been discovered. So, in the spring of 1927, all his parents could do was put Gaylord to bed for several weeks. The Nelsons waited. They worried and hoped that their son would soon get well. Fortunately, he did.

While Gaylord was recovering, he could hardly stand to miss all the fun that he was used to. His father tried to ease Gaylord's longing for the outdoors. One day he brought home an injured owl that he had found in the woods. Gaylord helped to mend the owl's broken wing and nursed it back to health. Dr. Nelson was right. Bringing an outdoor creature into his son's room helped to lift Gaylord's spirits.

rheumatic: roo **mat** ik

15

The many letters Gaylord received from his classmates at Clear Lake Elementary also helped to cheer him. When his fifth-grade class was preparing for an end-of-the-year school picnic, several of Gaylord's classmates wrote to him. Helen Hanna wrote: "Miss Larson said she bet you'd be there if you had to walk on crutches to get there." Although no one seems to know if Gaylord made it to the picnic, the letters helped him realize that he was missed.

Getting through his illness may have helped Gaylord develop

WHI IMAGE ID 65299

On May 6, 1927, a classmate wrote this letter to Gaylord while he was recovering from rheumatic fever.

the strength of character that would later help him through other difficulties. Some people become stronger when they are forced to face a hard time in their lives. Gaylord was one of those people.

A classroom in Clear Lake Elementary, 1925. Gaylord is seated in the front row, third from the left.

Politics was another important seed sown in Gaylord's youth. His parents were very interested and active in their local community. But their interests and concerns stretched beyond Clear Lake. At home, the Nelsons spent a lot of time

17

talking about which leaders would do the most to help the people in the state and country.

Mary and Anton Nelson chose to work hard for a **progressive** group within the **Republican Party**. One of the progressive leaders whom they most admired was Robert M. La Follette Sr. He was called "Fighting Bob" because he battled for the rights of all people, young and old, rich and poor. He believed that the government had stopped working for the average person. Bob La Follette fought for child labor laws, that is, laws to protect young children from working in factories and mines under terrible conditions. He also spoke out for equal rights for women, African Americans, and Jewish Americans.

The Nelson family believed in the values that Fighting Bob stood for. So did many others in Wisconsin. Bob La Follette was so popular that he became a **United States representative**, governor of the state, and finally a United States senator. Fighting Bob died in 1925, when he was still serving his term in the **Senate**. Gaylord saw that his own parents and their

progressive: in favor of positive change   **Republican Party**: one of the 2 main political parties in the United States   **United States representative**: person elected to Congress to speak or act for a particular region
Senate: in the federal government, the house of Congress where the states are represented equally. In state government, districts are represented equally in the Senate.

friends were very sad and upset to
have lost such a strong leader. By 1926,
Fighting Bob's son, known as "Young
Bob," won election to his father's vacant
Senate seat and carried on his father's
fight for the people of the state.

Fighting Bob La Follette was
Gaylord's early inspiration.

When Gaylord was 10 years old,
he went with his father to hear Young
Bob La Follette give a speech in Amery,
Wisconsin. In those days, politicians gave grand speeches
from the back platform of a train that pulled into stations
throughout the state. These **whistle-stop** events drew people
from all over the town and its surroundings.

In Amery, people crowded all around the caboose of the
train to hear what Young Bob had to say. As he spoke of
trying to help people improve their lives with better working
conditions, people waved their arms and cheered. After the
speech, Gaylord told his father that he knew what he wanted
to do when he was an adult. He wanted to be like Senator

whistle-stop: a railroad station where someone running for political office would make speeches to the people
of the town

19

La Follette. Gaylord realized he would like to go into politics.

Much later in his life Gaylord told a reporter at the *Wisconsin State Journal*, "I was afraid [Senator La Follette] was going to solve all the problems and I wouldn't have anything to do when I grew up." What Gaylord didn't know as a child was that he would someday follow in the footsteps of the La Follettes. He, too, would be elected to serve his state and his country. And, in the La Follette tradition, he would speak out strongly for what he believed in.

The La Follettes' goals as lawmakers were not so different from Anton Nelson's work as a doctor. All 3 men were devoting their lives to helping people, each in his own way. So, Gaylord followed his father's footsteps, too. He also found his own way to help people.

Gaylord took his first **political** action at the age of 12. That's when he traveled with his father to Eau Claire, Wisconsin. As they entered the city, Gaylord noticed that the main street was lined with enormous old trees that formed a graceful arch over the middle of the road. Gaylord thought it would be a

political (puh **lit** uh kuhl): having to do with the way a city, state, or nation governs itself

great idea if Clear Lake also planted trees on its main street to welcome visitors as they approached the town. He decided that he would speak to the Clear Lake City Council to propose his idea.

So, a short time later, Gaylord stood before the members of the council board. He suggested that the town ask Boy Scouts and Girl Scouts to plant the trees. That way the project wouldn't cost too much. But Gaylord's idea failed to win approval. Maybe the board members didn't take Gaylord's suggestion seriously, because it came from such a young person. The trees may not have been planted in Clear Lake, but many years later his idea grew into something much larger.

By the time Gaylord entered Clear Lake High School, he was still more interested in being outside than sitting in the classroom. Fortunately, he was smart enough to get by without studying very hard. In a postcard that he sent to his mother when she was away on a trip, he proudly wrote, "I got high marks in my six weeks exams. My lowest mark was 82." He then added some eye-popping news: "I took the car all by myself."

Probably the most important skills Gaylord learned during high school came from his activities outside of the classroom. He played the trumpet in the band and was chosen captain of his football and basketball teams. In these roles, he needed to work well with others,

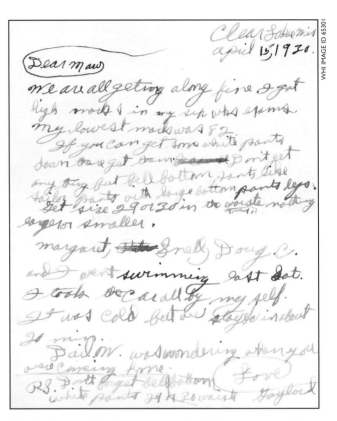

Gaylord was full of surprises. At 13, he wrote to his mother, "I took the car all by myself."

be part of a group effort, and develop leadership skills. All of those abilities came easily to Gaylord. They would see him through some tough battles later in his life.

Gaylord played football in high school. He is second from left in the front row.

Gaylord played the trumpet in the Clear Lake High School band.

Gaylord was respectful of each of his 38 classmates at Clear Lake High School. They returned that respect by choosing him to give their graduation speech in 1934. But even someone as easygoing as Happy Nelson got the last-minute jitters about speaking in front of his classmates and their families. On the day of the graduation he pretended to be sick. He did not attend the **ceremony**. Gaylord had no idea then that he would one day give hundreds of speeches that would help to change the country.

ceremony (**ser** uh moh nee): a formal event held to celebrate an important occasion, such as a wedding, graduation, or presidential inauguration

At college, Gaylord had a rough start. He tried out 2 different small schools in Wisconsin. He soon realized that he had not gained the skills to be a good college student. He may have felt that he was not yet ready to study very hard and concentrate in class. Gaylord ended up returning home to Clear Lake in 1935.

He took a job with the federal **Works Progress Administration (WPA)**. The WPA was a program that was set up by President Franklin D. Roosevelt in 1935. It employed many people who were out of work during very hard times in this country called the **Great Depression**. After a year of shoveling gravel for road construction, Gaylord decided that he was ready to leave his home in Clear Lake. He would try college once again.

During the Great Depression, many people found jobs with the Works Progress Administration.

Works Progress Administration (ad min uh **stray** shuhn) **(WPA):** a national program of projects such as building roads and bridges; designed to accomplish needed tasks as well as to put people back to work during the Great Depression   **Great Depression** (di **presh** uhn): an event during the 1930s, when many people lost their jobs and homes, and people all over the United States and other countries suffered

Works Progress Administration (WPA)

When Gaylord returned to Clear Lake after his first tries at college, he was lucky to get a job with the Works Progress Administration. Jobs were scarce in the mid-1930s due to the Great Depression. Many people were out of work and hungry. After Franklin D. Roosevelt became president in 1933, he began the WPA to help put people back to work. Like Gaylord, roughly 8.5 million people went to work restoring damaged roads, bridges, and school buildings and completing other projects throughout the country. In return, the workers earned some money to help put food on the table. The WPA continued until 1943. More than 4 million young people and high school students were given part-time jobs by the National Youth Administration, which was closely connected with the WPA.

This time Gaylord traveled 2,000 miles away to San Jose, California, to attend San Jose State College. That was farther away from Clear Lake than he had ever been before. Gaylord's 2 older sisters, Janet and Peg, had already attended San Jose State College. Their aunt Gertrude was a voice teacher there. She had offered to let Gaylord live in her home while he attended classes.

He wanted to go to college, but he still wasn't sure that he would be able to handle it. Had the break from school made him ready to work harder? Would he be able to live in a big city? After all, the number of students attending San Jose State College was 5 times bigger than the entire population of Clear Lake.

Gaylord decided that he had to try. He paid more attention in class and forced himself to study. What a surprise it was for him at the end of his first year to find out that he had made straight As! Gaylord received such high grades that he graduated from college with honors. While some accomplishments came easily to Gaylord, he had learned that sometimes he had to work very hard to achieve his goals.

WHI IMAGE ID 5904

Gaylord with his mother at his graduation from San Jose State College

3

The Seeds Take Root

When Gaylord returned to Clear Lake after graduation, his interest in politics was still very much alive. He thought that if he was serious about going into politics, he should know a lot about the laws that governed the state and the country. So he enrolled in law school at the University of Wisconsin in Madison. There, his path crossed with Robert M. La Follette Jr., who had inspired 10-year-old Gaylord with his speech at the Amery train station. Gaylord still remembered how he had watched Young Bob excite the cheering crowd with his ideas.

As Gaylord entered law school, Bob La Follette Jr. was running for re-election to his United States Senate seat as a Progressive Party candidate. Under his leadership, the Progressive Party had broken off completely from the Republican Party in 1934. Gaylord was the president of the

WHI IMAGE ID 32459

Young Bob La Follette led Wisconsin's Progressive Party until 1946.

Young Progressives at the university. The Young Progressives were a group of enthusiastic students who believed in the Progressive Party ideals, including protecting workers' rights and **civil rights**.

Gaylord and his friends spent long hours working on Bob La Follette Jr.'s **campaign**. They would often go door-to-door to talk to people and leave information about what their candidate hoped to accomplish as a senator. They stayed up late at night mailing out flyers and telling people about what a good man Young Bob was. Gaylord was so excited to be taking part in real-life politics that he often forgot to attend his law school classes. Robert M. La Follette Jr. won the election in 1940. But Gaylord had a lot of catching up to do before he graduated with the rest of his law school class.

When Gaylord graduated from law school in June of 1942, the United States was at war with Japan and Germany. German

civil rights: the rights that all members of a society have to freedom and equal treatment under the law
campaign (kam **payn**): a period of time before an election when candidates try to get people to vote for them

dictator Adolf Hitler was the head of Germany's **Nazi** Party. Under his rule, Germany invaded many countries in Europe during World War II. Hitler also organized mass killings of certain groups of people that he did not approve of, especially Jews, gypsies, and other groups. Hitler's troops were rounding up innocent people and killing them in an effort to eliminate anyone who was not of pure German **ancestry**.

WHI IMAGE ID 5896

Gaylord graduated from law school at the University of Wisconsin in 1942.

Just 6 months before Gaylord completed law school, Japanese troops had bombed Pearl Harbor, Hawaii, an American military **base** in the Pacific Ocean. That led America to enter World War II.

dictator: someone who has complete control of a country, often ruling it unjustly   **Adolf Hitler** (**ay** dolf **hit** lur): a dictator who ruled Germany from 1933 to 1945   **Nazi** (**not** zee): describing the followers of Adolf Hitler, who wanted to rid Europe of Jews and other peoples they considered "impure"   **ancestry** (**an** ses tree): a person's relatives, going back far in the past   **base**: a center that supports a military operation, including training people for military duties

World War II

By the time Gaylord graduated from law school in 1942, World War II had spread throughout many countries in Europe. The war began when Nazi Germany invaded Poland in 1939. Adolf Hitler, the head of the German Nazi Party, planned to make Germany the most powerful country in the world by attacking and taking over many other countries. Japan joined with Germany, fighting the war in Asia. Japan attacked a U.S. naval base on Hawaii's Pearl Harbor on December 7, 1941. The United States declared war on Japan. Four days later on December 11, Germany declared war on the United States.

In 1945, Gaylord was sent to the Pacific island of Okinawa to help American troops fight the Japanese and care for the wounded American soldiers. However, the battle of Okinawa was over by the time he arrived. The war officially ended 6 weeks after Gaylord arrived in Japan. The United States and its major **allies**, Great Britain, France, and the former Union of Soviet Socialist Republics (USSR), had won the war.

Gaylord felt that it was his responsibility to help fight in the war. Soon after he graduated, he signed up for the United States Army. Gaylord was sent to an army hospital in Denver,

ally (**al I**): person or country that gives support to another

Colorado. By then, veterans of the war were coming home with injuries that needed attention. Gaylord was trained to take X-rays.

He later entered **Officer Candidate School** and graduated with the rank of **second lieutenant**. Gaylord was then sent off to a training base called Indiantown Gap Military Reservation in Pennsylvania. There he was assigned to train a **company** of African American soldiers. At that time, African American troops were **segregated** from white troops, even though everyone was fighting for the same cause.

Gaylord soon realized that his men were forced to stay in the worst **barracks** on the army base. They had little heating. The beds were old, and some of the walls were rotting. His men were not allowed to use the swimming pool, sports fields, or other places where the white men went to relax. Gaylord saw that the African American soldiers under his command were given far less praise than their fellow white soldiers received for equal efforts.

Officer Candidate School: where people are trained to become officers in the military
second lieutenant (loo **ten** uhnt): an entry-level officer in the United States military   **company**: a unit of soldiers   **segregated**: separated for the purpose of keeping groups apart based on the color of their skin
barrack (**ber** uhk): building or buildings where soldiers live

31

Up until that time, Gaylord had known little about **discrimination**. Only one African American family had lived in Clear Lake when he was growing up. When Gaylord and an African American officer became good friends, Gaylord learned a lot. He was amazed to discover that his friend was not allowed to go into the same restaurants and hotels that Gaylord was.

African American soldiers faced discrimination and segregation despite their equal efforts. These soldiers rescued a drowning Marine and narrowly escaped death themselves.

His experience in the army made him vow that he would someday help to change things. And, as you will see, he did.

discrimination (dis krim uh **nay** shuhn): unfair treatment of people based on differences such as race, age, gender, or place of birth

32

4

Beginning a New Life

Gaylord met his future wife, Lieutenant Carrie Lee Dotson, while he was at Indiantown Gap. Carrie Lee was a nurse who had volunteered to use her skills at the army hospital where Gaylord was stationed. She was an energetic, no-nonsense young lady who got Gaylord's attention with her lively spirit.

Carrie Lee came from a poor town in rural Virginia. Her father died when she was 3 years old. After that, her mother didn't have enough money to raise all 10 of the children in her family. When Carrie Lee was 7 years old, she was sent to live in a home for poor children. There she was well taken care of and educated until she finished high school.

When Carrie Lee met Gaylord she thought he was handsome and smart. Gaylord was attracted to Carrie Lee's flashing blue eyes and her sense of humor. He liked the fact that she wasn't afraid to say what was on her mind. They went on several dates, but soon Gaylord received orders to ship overseas to Okinawa, an island in the Pacific Ocean. The 2 parted, never expecting to meet again.

Three soldiers from Wisconsin and Illinois operate a machine gun during World War II.

Five months after Gaylord arrived at his new base, a ship of nurses arrived at Okinawa to care for the wounded soldiers. Carrie Lee Dotson was among them. When the war was over, each of them was shipped back to

Carrie Lee Dotson and Gaylord Nelson were sent to the island of Okinawa during World War II. Here, Marines unload supplies on Okinawa in 1945.

the United States. This time, Carrie Lee and Gaylord agreed to meet again.

34

When Gaylord was released from the military, he still wanted to go into politics. By that time, La Follette's Progressive Party was beginning to **disband**. Some of the members were returning to the Republican Party, which was then the most popular political party in Wisconsin. Others were joining the **Democratic Party**.

Gaylord returned to Clear Lake and decided to run for the **legislature**. He campaigned for the Wisconsin State **Assembly** on the Republican ticket. He was defeated.

But there was a bright spot in Gaylord's plans. He and Carrie Lee had kept their promise to meet again when they each returned home. They were married on November 15, 1947, 2 years after the war had ended.

The Nelsons settled into an apartment in Madison, Wisconsin. Their Greenbush neighborhood was known as "the Bush" to people around town. The Bush had a mixture of different kinds of people—Italian and Jewish families, African Americans, and university students. It was a friendly neighborhood where the aromas of bubbling spaghetti

disband: to break up as a group or organization   **Democratic Party**: one of the 2 main political parties of the United States   **legislature** (**lej** uh slay chur): an elected group of people who have the power to make laws for the city, state, or nation   **assembly**: one house of the state legislature

sauce, baking **challah**, and simmering ham bone soup might mingle together in the air. This mix of people living in the neighborhood suited the young married couple very well.

Madison's Greenbush neighborhood was full of interesting sights and aromas. Here, an Italian woman prepares tomato paste.

In Madison, Gaylord returned to his interest in politics. This time he decided he would run for the state senate as a Democrat. He felt that the Democratic Party's goals were more similar to his own. In 1948, at age 32, he won the election. This was no easy task, because the Wisconsin Democrats had just begun to re-form as a modern party in May of the same year. When Gaylord won the election, he was one of only 3 Democrats in the state senate. There were 27 Republicans. It would take much effort to achieve any of his goals.

One of Gaylord's first goals as a state senator was to try and change the unfair segregation practices that he had

challah (**kah** luh *or* **hah** luh): a rich, eggy bread, usually braided, that is often served on the Jewish Sabbath or holidays

seen in the army. He introduced a **bill** into the state senate to **integrate** the Wisconsin **National Guard**. Unfortunately, there were not enough "yes" votes to make the bill a law. But when a Republican congressman introduced the exact same bill in the assembly it passed **unanimously**.

Gaylord did not receive credit for the change in the law, but he certainly played a big role in making it happen. After 1949 the Wisconsin National Guard became fully integrated. Later, in 1951, Gaylord Nelson was able to push through a law that expanded equal rights in the state. That law made it illegal to discriminate against people on the basis of their color, national origin, ancestry, or faith.

Carrie Lee and Gaylord in the 1950s

In the 10 years that Gaylord served in the Wisconsin legislature, many changes took place in the Nelson household. The family moved to a home in the new Crestwood

bill: a written proposal for a new law, to be discussed and voted on by lawmakers   **integrate** (in tuh grayt): to make facilities or organizations open to people of all races and ethnic groups   **National Guard**: standby military units that can be called into service by federal or state governments   **unanimously** (yoo **nan** i muhs lee): with everyone's agreement

neighborhood on Madison's west side. There they joined a group of like-minded, **activist** neighbors.

In 1953, their first child, Gaylord Anton Jr., was born. He was given the nickname "Happy," just as his father had been called as a young boy. Three years later, Happy's sister Cynthia ("Tia") came along. Once again, the family had to move into larger quarters. They settled in another home in the same Madison neighborhood.

While all the changes were taking place in the Nelson home, Gaylord continued to work hard to make improvements in the state. But he knew that if he wanted to accomplish more, he would need to move beyond the state

The Nelson kids enjoying wildlife with their father.

senate. In 1954, he ran for U.S. Congress but was defeated by the **incumbent**. Not one to give up, he decided to run for Wisconsin governor in 1957.

activist: someone who works to produce political or social change   **incumbent** (in **kum** bent): someone currently holding an office or position

Government Structure in the U. S.

The United States government and the state governments are structured in similar ways. Both are made up of 3 branches, so that no group will have too much power over another.

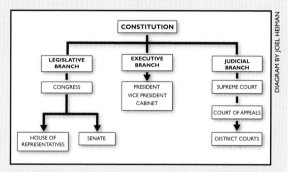

The United States government is made up of three branches: executive, legislative, and judicial.

The legislative branch, or Congress, is the law-making branch of government. Its responsibility is creating laws for everyone in the country to follow.

The executive branch of the United States is headed by the president, who has the responsibility to make sure all the laws of the country are carried out. In state government, the executive branch is headed by the governor.

The **judicial** branch has the responsibility to solve the problems that come up as people disagree on what the law means. Their solutions are called judgments. The Supreme Court is the head of the judicial branch. It is made up of 9 judges. The Wisconsin State Supreme Court has 7 judges.

---

judicial (joo **dish** uhl): to do with a court of law or a judge   **cabinet**: a group of people who advise the head of state, such as the president   **court of appeals**: the second level in the federal judicial system, also known as circuit court   **district court**: the lowest level trial court in the judicial system

5

Governor Gaylord Nelson

In 1957, Senator Nelson began his campaign for governor. He spoke out all across the state for the things he believed in. He wanted a good education for all children and equal rights for all citizens. He also wanted to preserve the environment. This goal—protecting the environment—was something he would work for until the end of his life.

By this time, Gaylord had not lived in Clear Lake for many years. But he had never forgotten the times he spent in the outdoors there. The natural beauty of Wisconsin's clear blue lakes and unspoiled forests had given him a deep love of nature.

Gaylord wanted to preserve such areas in Wisconsin for everyone to enjoy. But he saw that **developers** were buying more and more of the land in the state. The developers were

developer (di **vel** uh pur): person who plans and builds buildings and communities

cutting down forests to build homes and businesses in once-open **recreation areas**. Developers also polluted lakes. Parks were becoming overcrowded.

Gaylord understood that each part of the environment depends on the others. The closely woven connection between the air, water, land, and living things is called the **ecosystem**. On the campaign trail, he explained that all natural resources needed to be protected in order to create a **sustainable**, lasting environment. He warned that we could not support our planet if we did not take care of each part of it.

Gaylord wanted to know the concerns of people all over the state. Here he talks with Wisconsin farmers.

recreation (rek ree **ay** shun) **area**: place where activities are meant to be enjoyed, like sports or games or fishing or swimming   **ecosystem** (ee koh sis tuhm): a community of animals and plants that depend on each other and their environment   **sustainable**: lasting for long periods of time

After hundreds of speeches throughout the state, Gaylord Nelson won the election in November of 1958. He was the second Democrat ever to serve as governor of Wisconsin. Unfortunately, the happiness he felt at winning the election was mixed with personal sadness.

During the campaign, his father, Anton, had become very ill. While he was sick, Dr. Nelson had reminded his son of that ride home from Amery, when 10-year-old Gaylord had announced that he wanted to follow in the La Follettes' footsteps. Dr. Nelson died shortly after Gaylord won the election, but he had been happy to know that Gaylord's boyhood wish was about to come true.

The governor's inauguration was a very formal event. Still, Gaylord wore a suit instead of a tuxedo.

On January 5, 1959, Governor Gaylord Nelson was **inaugurated**. Every other governor before Gaylord had worn a tuxedo for the ceremony swearing him

inaugurated (in **awg** yoor ayt ed): sworn into office with a formal ceremony

42

There were advantages to being governor.

into office. But Gaylord chose to wear a black suit. Tuxedos "make me look too much like a penguin," the new governor told a reporter for the *Wisconsin State Journal*. Although Gaylord had left behind his small hometown, in some ways he remained the boy who was most comfortable dressed for tromping through the woods.

Once Gaylord became governor, there were very big changes for the whole Nelson family. Five-year-old Happy and 2-year-old Tia had never seen a house as big as the **governor's mansion** before. They couldn't believe that they had so many rooms to play in. Their dog, Wags, had plenty of new space to

governor's mansion (**man** shuhn): a special home owned by the state where its governor lives

43

run in, too. But the size and **luxury** of the governor's mansion did not change the family's informal lifestyle.

Gaylord's work in politics often required him to be away from home when his daughter, Tia, was growing up. But she says that he left a strong **imprint** on her life. "Papa was a **wordsmith**," she recalls. "As a young girl I would earn a nickel for every new word I could learn and use in a sentence."

Gaylord also taught Tia that people gained knowledge only when they admitted they did not know something. "One of the things that he repeated over and over for me was to never be afraid to say, I don't know," Tia remembers. She is still grateful for that lesson, which she has carried into her adult life.

The Nelsons lived at the governor's mansion at 99 Cambridge Road while Gaylord was in office.

luxury (**luhk** shur ee): expensive and beautiful surroundings that make life comfortable and pleasant
imprint: a strong influence or lasting effect on someone or something   **wordsmith**: someone who uses words well

Tia Nelson

Gaylord's daughter, Tia Nelson, has followed in her father's footsteps when it comes to caring deeply about the public lands of Wisconsin. She serves as executive secretary of the Wisconsin Board of **Commissioners** of Public Lands. The **agency** was formed to manage the money that came from the sale of the state's public lands. For example, your school library may have received money from the public lands trust fund that was set up by the Board of Commissioners. Much of the trust fund money

Tia followed in her father's footsteps. She now works to **conserve** Wisconsin's natural resources.

has gone to support state school libraries. In addition, the agency contributes to the protection of forests and natural areas in the state. Like her father, Tia continues to work hard so that land is used wisely.

commissioner (kuh **mish** uh nur): a person in charge of solving a particular problem or doing certain tasks
agency (**ay** juhn see): office or business that provides services to the public   **conserve**: to save something from loss or decay

45

Gaylord did more than create a love for learning in his children. He also kept his playful side. One night, when Governor Nelson was entertaining a visitor at the mansion, young Happy and his sister decided to get some attention. First they filled some balloons with water. Then they staked out a perch at the top of the winding staircase, where they had a perfect view of their father and his guest below. As the governor and his visitor stood quietly talking, balloons suddenly began to fly from overhead. Water splattered all over the floor where the governor and his surprised visitor were standing. Governor Nelson apologized to the man, but his children thought they saw a twinkle in their father's eye. Maybe

PHOTO COURTESY OF TIA NELSON

The Nelsons in the governor's mansion. Behind them is the staircase where Tia and Happy threw water balloons.

at that very moment he was remembering the cow in the banker's house.

Cars began to clutter the highways in the 1950s.

Although Gaylord Nelson never lost his sense of humor or playful spirit, he was very serious about his job as Wisconsin's thirty-fifth governor.

In the late 1950s, when Gaylord became governor, the population of the country was growing quickly. Most people were earning enough money to buy cars. Manufacturers made bigger and faster cars to fill the demand. The government was paving more highways. All of this made it possible for more and more people to travel from the crowded big cities to **recreational** parks and camping grounds for vacations. Unfortunately, the once wide-open spaces were becoming crowded, too. Tents and trailers were jammed up against each other. Motorboats buzzed through clean lakes, leaking gas into the once crystal clear water.

Gaylord could see how people were beginning to destroy the natural beauty of the land. He told legislators of the state

recreational (rek ree **ay** shuh nuhl): done or used for pleasure or relaxation

47

that it was "now or never." If everyone did not take steps to halt the growing problem, it would soon be too late.

Then he took action. One of the first steps Gaylord took was to create the Department of Resource Development. The role of this agency was to plan for future growth in the state. Rather than allowing homes to spring up all over rural areas, the department proposed planned communities that included green spaces and preserved recreation areas.

The St. Croix River is one of many natural resources Gaylord fought to preserve.

After Governor Nelson was elected to a second term in 1960, he created the Outdoor Recreation Action Program. This program allowed the state to set aside funds to buy lands that would preserve Wisconsin's outdoor

48

resources for generations to come. If you've ever visited the Apostle Islands, camped in Governor Dodge State Park, hiked the Ice Age Trail, or swum in the clear lakes of northern Wisconsin, you can thank Gaylord Nelson for making sure that you could. This program was so popular that Democrats and Republicans alike supported it. It earned Gaylord Nelson the title of Wisconsin's "**Conservation** Governor."

The Apostle Islands are another area Gaylord helped to preserve. Many people visit the islands each year.

conservation (kon sur **vay** shuhn): protection of valuable things such as forests, wildlife, and natural resources from change, loss, or damage

49

6

Moving on to Washington

In the early 1960s, the entire country was badly in need of environmental reform. Washing detergents with harmful **phosphates** were running into the lakes. These pollutants were killing off fish and other important underwater life. People were cutting down large areas of forests without any plans for regrowth. Governor Nelson decided that he might be able to do more for the country's worsening environmental problems if he ran for the United States Senate.

Most people in Wisconsin knew of Gaylord Nelson's accomplishments as governor. The state's citizens and

phosphate (**fahs** fayt): a type of chemical

50

DAVID SANDELL

Young and old came out to cheer on Gaylord when he ran for the United States Senate.

legislators had come to trust him for his honesty and for the respect he showed toward his opponents. He was known as a man who might strongly disagree with someone but who would never use personal insults. Charles Clark, Gaylord's close friend from Clear Lake, once said, "He could **debate** you all day and never lose his temper."

By the time the campaign for the U.S. Senate was over, Gaylord had traveled throughout the state of Wisconsin. He met personally with many people in small rural towns and large cities. He listened to their needs and told them of his ideas. During these conversations, his friendly and natural manner made people feel as if he were their new friend. He won the election in November of 1962 and was inaugurated on January 8, 1963.

debate (duh **bayt**): to discuss between sides with different points of view

PHOTO COURTESY OF TIA NELSON

Gaylord's daughter, Tia, remembers how important reading and understanding words were to him.

By the time he was elected to the United States Senate, Gaylord and Carrie Lee had 3 children. Their youngest son, Jeffrey, had been born in 1961. Soon after the inauguration, Gaylord, Carrie Lee, Happy, Tia, and Jeffrey Nelson said good-bye to their dear friends in Madison. The young family packed up their belongings and traveled to Washington, D.C.

Carrie Lee recalls, "The car that Gaylord drove at that time was pretty old and not at all fancy." Soon after the Nelsons arrived in the capital city, Gaylord was driving in his car with another senator in the passenger seat. The other senator asked Gaylord to pull over into a lot filled with shiny new automobiles. There, on the spot, the senator offered to buy Gaylord a brand-new car.

As a U.S. senator, Gaylord visited people all over the state.

Gaylord thanked his new friend very much but immediately refused the offer. The Nelsons had come to live among the most powerful people in the country. Even though Gaylord and his fellow legislators would make laws that would affect the whole nation and the world, he remained a **modest** man. Just as he had turned down wearing a tuxedo at his inauguration for governor years earlier, he saw no reason to show off now.

Senator Nelson's strongest commitment was to the environment, but he continued to object whenever he saw injustice and unfair treatment. During the time he served in

modest (**mod** ist): not wanting to show off or draw attention to oneself

the U.S. Senate, the country was faced with both.

A fellow Wisconsinite, Joseph McCarthy of Appleton, had been elected to the United States Senate in 1946. While in the Senate, Senator

The Nelson family walking through Great Falls National Park in Great Falls, Virginia. Even Wags liked to hike.

McCarthy had used his powerful position to accuse many citizens of being **Communists** and **disloyal** to the United States government. Most often, his claims were false. But many innocent people were called before McCarthy's **investigating** committee. Though they had done nothing wrong, they often lost their jobs and the respect of those who believed Senator McCarthy's **accusations**. People were afraid to speak out against McCarthy's unfair bullying. Some feared that they would become the next victims.

Communist (**kom** yoo nist): person who supports a system of government in which businesses and property are controlled by the state   **disloyal**: not faithful to one's country, family, friends, or beliefs   **investigating**: finding out as much as possible about something or someone   **accusation** (ak yoo **zay** shuhn): claim that someone has done something wrong

Joseph McCarthy died in 1957. But other investigations carried on by the House Un-American Activities Committee (HUAC) continued into the mid-1970s as a result of McCarthy's finger-pointing. When Gaylord Nelson entered the Senate, he was not afraid to speak out against this continuing **abuse of power**. These investigations threatened "the very freedoms that most sharply **distinguish** our **democracy** from the Communist system," he said. Governor Nelson knew that the right to speak freely was one of the rights that made our country different from a Communist nation. Many others

in powerful positions agreed with him. The investigations were ended in 1975 as a result of the work of the National Committee to Abolish HUAC.

Senator Joseph McCarthy wrongly accused many people of disloyalty.

abuse of power: the use of a powerful position to do something illegal or improper   distinguish (dis **ting** gwish): mark someone or something as separate or different from others   democracy (di **mok** ruh see): a way of governing a country in which the people choose their own leaders in elections

Other injustices were still taking place in the 1960s. African Americans continued to face severe discrimination. In the South, they were not able to sit with white people on the public buses. Instead, they had to move to the back of the bus or stand. African Americans were also forced to use separate public bathrooms and restaurants. They had segregated theaters and drinking fountains. These were not nearly as nice as those reserved for white people.

And African American children were not allowed to attend the same schools as white children. The segregated schools had older buildings, books, and other equipment. On May 17, 1954, the Supreme Court had ruled that public schools could no longer be segregated. However, even after this ruling, several states still refused to integrate their schools.

WHI IMAGE ID 4993

Activists battled to break down the barriers of segregation.

Gaylord fought hard to improve conditions for African American people. Some Democrats warned Gaylord that he was pushing too quickly for changes that were still unpopular in the country. Once again, Gaylord showed that he was not afraid to stand up for something he believed in. He was proud to be a cosponsor of the most powerful civil rights bill ever to be signed in the Senate. Ten years after the 1954 Supreme Court case, the Civil Rights Act of 1964 finally enforced **racial integration** in all public places, including schools. That year, African American students were protected from angry white crowds as they entered all-white schools throughout the South. Enforced school integration was an important step in the battle for African American equality.

During the same period, Gaylord Nelson took another unpopular position that turned out to be right. In the early 1960s, the United States became involved in the Vietnam War.

In 1965, President Lyndon Johnson asked the United States Senate to vote on spending $700 million dollars more to fight the war. Senator Nelson stood with 2 other senators in

racial integration (**ray** shuhl in tuh **gray** shuhn): the end of the practice of keeping groups apart based on the color of their skin

objecting. He voted against the request. "Obviously you need my vote less than I need my **conscience**," he told his fellow senators.

Vietnam War

The United States participated in the Vietnam War from 1959 to April 30, 1975, in Southeast Asia. The war occurred in Vietnam, Laos, and Cambodia. The goal of the war was to stop South Vietnam from falling into the hands of a Communist system of government, a form of government that our country opposed. Thousands of American and Vietnamese soldiers, as well as innocent **civilians**, were killed in the war. Billions of dollars were spent. And still our country had failed to help South Vietnam to set up an independent government.

The country spent billions of dollars more. Many more lives were lost. Finally, in March of 1973, the United States withdrew all troops from Vietnam although the war did not officially end until 1975. Senator Nelson was later praised for his wisdom in speaking out against the war. Though he

conscience (**kon** shuhns): an inner feeling of what is right and what is wrong   **civilian** (si **vil** yuhn): someone who is not in armed forces such as the army, navy, or air force

had strongly disagreed with his fellow legislators on several issues, he always treated his opponents with respect. When

a Washington magazine asked legislators whom they most enjoyed working with, Gaylord Nelson's name rose to the top of the list.

Gaylord Nelson never stopped fighting for civil

Gaylord often spoke to crowds during the years he served in the Wisconsin and United States governments.

rights and justice. Yet conservation of the country's natural resources was still his major concern. He told his fellow senators, "Unless this nation **girds** for battle immediately, its people are not going to have clean water to drink, clean air to breathe, decent soil in which to grow their food, and a green outdoors in which to live a few decades from now."

girds (gurdz): prepares for a difficult job

His actions reflected his beliefs. One of the first things he had done as U.S. senator was to cosponsor a bill to create a **Youth Conservation Corps**. Thousands of young people were **recruited** to help plant trees and clean up parks and recreation areas. In a short time, the young people of the country began to make a difference. The Youth Conservation Corps was not unlike Gaylord's boyhood idea of asking boys and girls to plant trees along the main street of Clear Lake. His youthful plan had been the first glimmer of what was to become a successful nationwide program.

Senator Nelson continued to sponsor and cosponsor many environmental bills that became law. But he needed help to convince the country that our water, air, and land were in danger if all people didn't do their share to protect those natural resources. Gaylord called on the new president, John F. Kennedy, for assistance. In August of 1963, he wrote a letter to President Kennedy asking him to make the environment one of his main concerns. "There is no domestic issue more important to America in the long-run than the conservation and proper use of our natural resources," he wrote.

Youth Conservation Corps (cor): a national program that put young people to work on projects that helped to keep our natural resources healthy, including planting trees and working in parks   **recruited** (ree **kroo** tid): called upon to serve in the military or to be part of a group or cause

Gaylord urged President Kennedy to visit Wisconsin for a tour of the Apostle Islands in the northern part of the state. Sure enough, a little more than a month after Gaylord sent his letter, President Kennedy left Washington, D.C., for a 5-day tour of conservation areas in 11 different states.

May 24, 1963

Hon. John F. Kennedy
The White House
Washington, D. C.

Dear Mr. President:

Thank you for your letter respecting the subject matter of conservation.

I did talk with Arthur Schlesinger about some ideas which it seemed to me might be useful in dramatizing your concern for the conservation of our natural resources. I am jotting some notes and will send along to you a memo.

If it appears to you that it may be of some value to have a discussion, I would certainly appreciate the opportunity to talk with you.

Sincerely yours,

GAYLORD NELSON
U. S. Senator

GN:dd

Note: The ORIGINAL of this document has been sent to the Clear Lake Area Historical Museum, Clear Lake, Wisconsin, for display in the Gaylord Nelson Room.

Special display -- Senator Nelson's correspondence with President John F. Kennedy, respecting the President's conservation tour (1963).

Gaylord urged President Kennedy to make the environment a priority.

Gaylord's good friend Martin Hanson flew the helicopter that guided President Kennedy from place to place. As the helicopter landed in Ashland, Wisconsin, Hanson recalls, "Buses of school children were lined up on the highway. Bands were playing. And the mayor was there, standing on a platform made of big timbers."

"If properly developed, . . . recreational areas here can provide enjoyment for many millions of people for many years to come," Kennedy told the cheering crowd. The newspapers picked up on the president's words. Having the popular President Kennedy on his side helped Gaylord take on future environmental battles.

CAPITAL NEWSPAPERS

President Kennedy and Gaylord discuss Gaylord's plans for the environment.

In 1964 the United States government voted the Wilderness Act into law. Like the Outdoor Recreation Action Program, the Wilderness Act allowed the government to buy up and protect many acres of land for hiking and outdoor recreation.

The Apostle Islands National Lakeshore is one of Wisconsin's scenic treasures. Part of it is now called the Gaylord Nelson Wilderness.

63

Recreational Trails

Gaylord helped preserve miles of land for hiking and recreation. These are some of the United States' protected areas. The **Appalachian** Trail is a 2,175-mile hiking trail that runs from

These trails are protected for recreational use.

Georgia to Maine. The Pacific Crest Trail is a mountainous hiking and horse-riding trail that runs for 2,650 miles from the Mexican to Canadian border in the western United States. The North Country Trail stretches across 7 states, from New York to North Dakota. At 4,600 miles long, the trail is the longest hiking path in the United States. The Ice Age Trail is a footpath of more than 1,000 miles that crosses Wisconsin from Door County in the east to Polk County in the west. This scenic trail runs along the edge of an area that was covered with glacial ice 12,000 years ago.

Appalachian (ap uh **lay** chuhn)

When Gaylord's first 6-year term in the U.S. Senate was up, he knew that there was still much to do. He decided to run for a second term in 1968. He remembered how he had been inspired when candidate Bob La Follette Jr. rolled into Amery, Wisconsin, on the train and spoke to the people. So, he decided to do the same thing during his campaign. And he won.

In addition to helping to protect the land, air, and water around us, Gaylord Nelson helped to protect us from dangers to our own health. After all, we humans and other animals are an important

PHOTO COURTESY OF TIA NELSON

Following in the La Follette tradition, the Nelsons campaigned on the back of a train that stopped throughout Wisconsin.

65

part of the whole ecosystem. He fought to place warnings on medicines that could be harmful. He also worked to ban dangerous chemicals used to kill pests, such as **DDT**. DDT was used to kill mosquitoes and other pests. During the summers of the 1940s and 1950s, it was not at all unusual for children to watch large trucks spraying heavy clouds of DDT into the streets where they were playing baseball or capture the flag.

DDT has been banned since 1974 because it caused harm to other animals and may have been harmful to humans.

It wasn't easy for Gaylord to convince people of the dangers of DDT. This advertisement promises that DDT "kills insects and [is] safe to use."

DDT: Dichloro-Diphenyl-Trichloroethane (dı **klawr** oh dı **fen** uhl trı klawr oh **eth** ayn)

DDT: Dichloro-Diphenyl-Trichloroethane

Scientists first created DDT in the 1870s, and in 1939 they discovered the chemical was an effective **pesticide**. DDT was then used during WWII to control mosquitoes that spread diseases such as malaria. After the war, cities began to use DDT heavily. In the late 1950s, scientists began to see that the pesticide was having bad effects on wildlife and fish. Birds were dying at a greater rate, and their eggshells were becoming thinner and less protective of their young. No one knew what effects DDT was having on human life, but studies began to show that pesticides might cause certain types of cancer.

In 1962, the author Rachel Carson published a book called *Silent Spring*, in which she explained what scientists were seeing. The book brought the problem of DDT to the attention of the American people.

The use of DDT became a very troublesome issue among scientists, the companies that made it, and lawmakers. In 1965, Senator Nelson proposed a nationwide ban on DDT. In 1970, through his efforts, Wisconsin was the first state in the country to ban DDT. Eventually, in 1972, use of DDT was banned in the entire United States. It is still used in some other countries.

pesticide: a chemical used to kill pests, such as insects

Unfortunately, throughout much of the 1960s, many people still did not understand the importance of their environment. They continued to behave in ways that harmed the water, land, and natural resources. Then, in 1969, there came a wake-up call. A ship off the coast of California had a huge oil spill. Millions of tons of black, thick liquid floated in the waters of the Pacific Ocean and oozed up onto the shore. The pollution caused by the spill was some of the worst ever seen. Fish, sea lions, ducks, birds, and other living creatures were unable to move as the slimy fluid coated their bodies. People from the area came to help by washing the oil from the helpless animals, but most of the wildlife died.

The careless destruction caused by the spill troubled Gaylord Nelson and many other Americans. People had begun to realize that pollution was still a big problem. Something more needed to be done, but Gaylord wasn't sure what it was.

Eventually he thought of a plan to get the people's attention. The idea came to him from the **teach-ins** about the

teach-in: a meeting held to teach a group of people about a particular issue

Vietnam War that were being held on college campuses. The teach-ins helped students learn more about the war. Many students found that the more they learned, the more they wanted the United States government to bring its soldiers home.

Gaylord Nelson saw how effective these teach-ins were. So he decided to help organize teach-ins on the environment throughout the country. He thought the best way to call attention to the environment would be to schedule all the teach-ins on the same day. That day would be called Earth Day.

7

Earth Day and Beyond

Gaylord Nelson hoped that Earth Day would spur people to think of a set of actions that would extend beyond protecting the outdoor environment. "Our goal is an environment of **decency**, quality and **mutual** respect for all human beings and all other living creatures—an environment without ugliness, without **ghettoes**, without poverty, without discrimination, without hunger, and without war," Nelson said. His vision was to make people aware of the chance for a better, safer life for all people of the Earth.

This newsletter announces the first Earth Day in 1970.

---

decency (**dee** suhn see): thoughtful, kind, or respectable behavior   **mutual** (**myoo** choo uhl): the same feelings shared by 2 or more people or groups   **ghetto** (**get** oh): a usually poor city neighborhood where people of the same race, religion, or ethnic background live, often not by choice

The first Earth Day was April 22, 1970. People had read about Gaylord's plans in newspapers all over the country. By then, it was clear that many individuals now shared Gaylord's concerns for the environment. But they didn't know what they could do. On that first Earth Day, more than 20 million people in the United States took part in learning, teaching, doing, and **demonstrating** for a cleaner, healthier place to live.

Earth Day volunteers plant a red oak tree.

Lawmakers talked about how to strengthen laws that would protect the environment. And children in schools all over the country pitched in to clean their parks and playgrounds.

After the first Earth Day, the national and state governments passed stronger environmental laws. The **Environmental Protection Agency**, or EPA, was formed. Its task was to see that

demonstrating: gathering with others in public to display feelings for or against something   **Environmental Protection Agency (EPA)**: a government organization formed in 1970 to enforce the laws protecting the environment

everyone paid attention to the laws that were made to help keep our environment clean. If a factory was burning **toxins** that were dirtying the air we breathe, it was up to the EPA to make sure that the factory stopped.

Environmental Protection Agency

After the first Earth Day in April 1970, private citizens and government leaders were more aware of the problems facing the environment. That year, Congress proposed the establishment of the Environmental Protection Agency (EPA) to create standards to help keep the environment clean and safe. President Richard Nixon signed the bill on December 2, 1970. Since then the EPA has employed thousands of scientists and environmental experts. They make environmental rules and ensure those rules are followed. Before the EPA existed, the government had no way to control pollutants. Thanks to Gaylord Nelson's work, today there are rules to protect our health and the environment we live in.

Everyone, from schoolchildren who cleaned up litter on the playground to President Nixon of the United States, was affected by Gaylord Nelson's warnings. Citizens—young and

toxin (**tok** suhn): any material that is harmful or poisonous old, city dwellers and people living in rural communities—began to take notice of natural resources that they once had taken for granted. Fewer people littered our highways and parkways with trash. Children from all over the country drew pictures and wrote letters to Senator Nelson. He organized many of those letters into a book that was called *What Are Me and You Gonna Do?* The title reflects the simple question that most citizens had on their minds.

The country still needed to do more to prevent factories from polluting our air and water. From 1970 to 1980, more laws to protect and conserve the environment were passed than had been passed in the previous 170 years. For that reason, the 1970s became known as the "Environmental Decade."

Many people wore buttons with the ecology symbol to show that they cared about the environment.

Children all over the country sent letters to Gaylord. This letter, from a fourth-grade student, appeared in Gaylord's book.

Dear Senator Nelson
    The way that you are handling the problem about pollution is okay with me. But I think you should have a little bit more action on Lake Monona and Mendota because they are just to polluted.
    Now how to solve this problem,
① you could scrap it off.
② you could send down skin diver's to cut it up.
③ you could cut it up then scrap it off.
    because I want to have some fun in our Lake's. So get to work right now!!!

                    from
                    David Maly

The Environmental Decade

The 10 years that followed the first Earth Day brought about many new laws that helped to protect the environment and human safety. As a result of the laws that were passed between 1970 and 1980, the use of toxins was controlled. The air became cleaner. The water became safer. In addition, forests were managed with the idea of replacing the trees that were cut for lumber. Lands were preserved for our recreation. **Endangered** fish and animals were better protected. Little did Gaylord Nelson know what the consequences of his Earth Day plan would be when the idea came to him. The 1970s showed that the effects were very powerful.

Two of the most important new laws were the **Clean Air Act** of 1970 and the **Clean Water Act** of 1972. But many other laws that would help to protect the Earth were enacted during the environmental decade.

Gaylord easily won a third term in the U.S. Senate, which began in 1974. Throughout the decade, he was a driving force in making environmental protection become a reality.

endangered: in danger of disappearing   **Clean Air Act**: a United States law to protect the air from pollution; first passed in 1967 as the Air Quality Act and amended in 1970 as the Clean Air Act   **Clean Water Act**: a United States law passed in 1972 to protect lakes, streams, and oceans from pollution

People now had cleaner water and air, and endangered animals and wilderness areas were protected, too.

Even though he did not win a fourth term in 1980, Gaylord Nelson was certainly not ready to stop his fight for a better environment. At age 65, he became **counselor** of the Wilderness Society. This organization devoted itself to keeping certain areas of the country in their natural state for people to enjoy.

Gaylord's days were still very full, but in many different ways. He continued to work on something that he believed in so strongly, but now he could spend more time with his family. He could also enjoy his hobbies. "That period of time gave me the opportunity to really spend some wonderful time with my dad," recalls Gaylord's youngest son, Jeff. "I would come home to Washington, D.C., on my summer vacations from college and Papa and I would do things together." Whether chopping vegetables for a Chinese dinner, hoeing the garden, or catching a prize at the end of a fishing line, Jeff enjoyed the rare opportunity to spend time with his father. He learned many

counselor (**koun** sil ur): someone who gives advice

lessons from his dad during this time. Jeff says, "Whenever I need to make a big decision in my life, I always try to imagine what Papa would do, and things usually turn out right."

Unfortunately, in the 1980s, citizens and lawmakers again began to get lazy about the environment. Fewer and fewer environmental laws were passed. Others were not strictly enforced. Pollution went unchecked. There was so much garbage that people didn't know what to do with it. **Landfill** sites were overflowing. People and animals were getting sick from the toxins in the air.

In 1990, another tanker off the coast of California dumped more oil into the ocean. Once again, beaches were covered. Animals and birds died as the oil coated their wings and fur. Thousands of fish lay dead upon the sand.

That year, Gaylord Nelson met with some

JULIE DERMANSKY

A worker cleans a bird after an oil spill.

landfill: garbage that is stacked and covered with earth

of the people who had helped organize Earth Day in 1970. It was time to get the attention of the people once again. They realized that what we do in this country affects people in other parts of the world and what they do affects us. So Gaylord thought it was important to involve all nations in learning the important lessons of caring for our planet. It would be a chance for people all over the world to recognize their common interest and to work together on a single goal.

PHOTO BY LEAH L. JONES. COPYRIGHT WISCONSIN STATE JOURNAL. REPRINTED WITH PERMISSION.

Elementary students throw away trash after cleaning a park for Earth Day.

On April 22, 1990, 200 million people from 141 nations joined in the Earth Day celebration. This was 10 times more than had taken part in the first Earth Day of 1970! Children in Central America planted thousands of fruit trees. People in Japan began to recycle garbage. Canadian citizens organized walks to pick up litter. Once again, schoolchildren learned how people everywhere could do their part.

Performers at an Earth Day rally sing about protecting the environment.

Not many events can bring together people of every faith and every nationality in a single **mission**, but Earth Day does. On that day, we are all part of one **global** society working to save our planet.

As the counselor of the Wilderness Society, Gaylord visited grade schools all over the country to speak to children. He felt that young people were the greatest hope for the future. Many of the students knew a lot about how to take care of the environment. They were thinking about what they could do as individuals. Gaylord was surprised and delighted to know that his Earth Day efforts were starting to pay off.

mission (**mish** uhn): a particular task given to a person or group to carry out   **global**: something that relates to the whole world

Students in Clear Lake prepared this bulletin board for Earth Day 2007.

Every year, Gaylord returned to the new elementary school in his hometown of Clear Lake. The people in the town were so proud of him that they named the school in his honor.

One year, when he was speaking to the first-grade class at the Gaylord A. Nelson Educational Center, a little boy raised his hand and asked, "Senator Nelson, how do you like being named after our school?" Gaylord just smiled and said that it felt very good.

Gaylord Nelson's accomplishments were recognized far beyond Clear Lake. In 1995, President Bill Clinton awarded him the **Presidential Medal of Freedom**, the highest honor that can be awarded to a civilian. "As the founder of Earth Day, he is the grandfather of all that grew out of that event—the Environmental Protection Act, the Clean Air Act, the Clean

Presidential (prez uh **den** shuhl) **Medal of Freedom**: an award given to someone who has served the country in an outstanding way

Water Act, the Safe Drinking Water Act," President Clinton said. "He also set a standard for people in public service to care about the environment and try to do something about it." The medal was a way of thanking Gaylord for his outstanding contribution to our country.

The new elementary school in Clear Lake was renamed for Gaylord.

President Clinton awarded Gaylord Nelson the Presidential Medal of Freedom for his outstanding contribution to our environment.

By Earth Day 2000, Gaylord Nelson was content that he had made a difference. In his Earth Day speech that year he said, "We have finally come to understand that the wealth of the nation is its air, water, soil, forests, minerals, rivers, lakes, oceans, scenic beauty, wildlife **habitats**, and **biodiversity**. Take this resource base away, and all that is left is a wasteland."

habitat: the place or environment where a plant or animal naturally or normally lives
biodiversity (bı oh duh **vur** suh tee): when a wide variety of plants and animals live in a single area

8

Carrying on Gaylord Nelson's Work

You may already know a lot of things that can be done to protect our environment. It's very possible that you have taken part in some sort of Earth Day activities in your school. In 2008, more than 100,000 schools around the country participated in celebrating Earth Day. Some had weeklong projects.

But taking care of our planet is more than a one-day or one-week activity. Those who helped Gaylord Nelson organize Earth Day understood that we must act to protect the Earth each day of the year. In 1994, the Earth Day **Network** was founded. The network keeps Gaylord Nelson's Earth Day vision and goals alive in its educational materials. It suggests ways that we can all do our part, all the time. You may be able to think of others. Keeping a planet healthy is a team effort, and every contribution matters.

network: a group of people who exchange information

Earth Day Network

One of the people who helped plan and organize the first Earth Day was a young law student by the name of Denis Hayes. He shared Gaylord Nelson's concern about the environment and decided to take a year of his life to help make Earth Day a reality in 1970. He also helped organize the worldwide Earth Day events in 1990. Since the first Earth Day Hayes has devoted himself to helping create tougher laws to protect the environment. He is also the director of the Earth Day Network (EDN). This is an organization that is dedicated to carrying on the accomplishments and ideals of Earth Day. One of EDN's major goals is to help boys and girls understand how they may continue to make our world a cleaner, safer, more environmentally friendly place. Here are some of EDN's suggestions.

TIME FOR A NAP

Set your computer on "sleep" mode when you're not using it.
Don't use screen savers. They use more energy.

PRECIOUS PAPER

Use both sides of the page.
Buy recycled paper.
Always throw away paper in a recycling bin.

FLIP THAT SWITCH

Be sure to turn lights off when no one is in the room.
Make stickers that remind you to "Flip the switch when leaving!"

Gaylord Nelson died on July 3, 2005, at the age of 89, but his **legacy** lives on. Every time you think about putting trash in a trash bin rather than throwing it on the ground, every time you make sure to recycle garbage rather than dumping it all in a landfill, every time you ride a bike rather than getting into a car, every time you turn out the lights before leaving a room, you, too, are being good **stewards** of the environment. Gaylord Nelson would be proud.

WHI IMAGE ID 56845

Gaylord takes time out from a campaign to chat with 2 boys.

legacy (**leg** uh see): something that is handed down from one generation to another   **steward** (**stoo** urd): person who assists or cares for something

Author's Note

I have taken great pleasure in writing about a man who did so much to make this Earth a better place. As I've seen my 8-year-old twin grandsons pick up stray trash from their local playground and place it in a trash bin, I know that I am witnessing the results of Gaylord Nelson's efforts to educate us all about our individual responsibility to our planet. We have come a long, long way in understanding how to care for our environment. But we still have work to do.

Scientists and **environmentalists** know that holes are being punctured in the protective **ozone** layer between the sun and the Earth. Our air conditioners and many types of spray cans create **chlorofluorocarbons (CFCs)** that float up into the air and cause the ozone layer to thin. As a result, we are exposed to harmful rays from the sun.

---

environmentalist: someone who works to protect the natural world   **ozone**: a form of oxygen that sits between the sun and Earth to protect the Earth from the sun's harmful rays
chlorofluorocarbons (**klawr** oh flawr oh **kahr** buhnz) (**CFCs**): a type of chemical compound, created by use of air conditioners and some spray cans, that floats up into the air and causes the ozone layer to thin

Another very large problem is **global warming** caused by the release of too much carbon dioxide into the atmosphere. Carbon dioxide is one of many "greenhouse gases." In the right balance with other gases in the air, carbon dioxide protects the Earth from becoming too cold. But when too much carbon dioxide is released into the atmosphere, the sun's rays are trapped above the Earth's surface, making things too warm on our planet.

As our Earth warms, our climate, the food we grow, the trees we plant, and the water that supplies our oceans, lakes, and streams will all be badly affected. When our family cars, our homes, and our factories guzzle up the Earth's limited supply of oil, coal, and other fossil fuels, they release fumes containing carbon dioxide. They not only make the Earth too hot but also pollute the air we breathe. Scientists and engineers have been working to create new ways of providing energy that will not cause harmful warming. **Renewable energy** sources such as wind and sun may someday fill our energy needs.

global warming: an apparent, gradual rise in the temperature of the Earth's atmosphere, caused by the greenhouse effect   **renewable energy**: power from sources that can never be used up, such as wind, waves, and the sun

In Gaylord Nelson's vision, the young people of today are the hope for the future. He was relying on you to learn, understand, care, and take action. Together, you are all capable of joining in to carry on Gaylord Nelson's work of preserving our planet for yourselves and future generations.

Appendix

In His Own Words

"As we think about the richness of the world in which we live—its forests, its clear blue waters, and all of its varied life forms—we must understand how our actions affect all of them."

ᕕ Gaylord Nelson, *Beyond Earth Day*

"We must recognize that we're all part of a web of life around the world. Anytime you extinguish a species, the consequences are serious."

ᕕ Gaylord Nelson

"Children are born loving the out-of-doors and are fascinated by birds, bugs and other animals and what they do. Tapping into that natural curiosity and building upon it to teach our youngsters about the natural world and how it works is one of the most important things we can do to help the environment in the future."

ᕕ Gaylord Nelson, *Beyond Earth Day*

Appendix

Gaylord's Time Line

1916 — Gaylord Anton Nelson is born in Clear Lake, Wisconsin, on June 4.

1934 — Gaylord graduates from Clear Lake High School.

1939 — Gaylord graduates from San Jose State College.

1942 — Gaylord graduates from University of Wisconsin Law School.

1942–1945 — Gaylord serves in the United States Army.

1946 — Gaylord runs for Wisconsin State Assembly as a progressive Republican but is defeated.

1947 — Gaylord marries Carrie Lee Dotson.

1948 — Gaylord wins election to the Wisconsin State Senate as a Democrat. He serves for 10 years.

1953 — Gaylord Anton (Happy) Nelson Jr. is born.

1954 — Gaylord runs for the United States Congress but is defeated.

1956 — Cynthia (Tia) Nelson is born.

1958 — Gaylord is elected Wisconsin governor. He serves 2 terms.

1961 — Jeffrey Nelson is born.

1962 — Gaylord is elected to the United States Senate. He serves 3 terms.

1963 — President Kennedy visits the Apostle Islands.

1970 — The first Earth Day is celebrated on April 22.

1980 — Gaylord loses the election to a fourth term in the U.S. Senate.

Gaylord becomes counselor of the Wilderness Society.

1990 — Worldwide Earth Day is celebrated.

1995 — Gaylord receives the Presidential Medal of Freedom.

2005 — Gaylord Nelson dies on July 3.

Glossary

Pronunciation Key

a   c<u>a</u>t (kat), pl<u>ai</u>d (plad),
    h<u>a</u>lf (haf)

ah   f<u>a</u>ther (**fah** THur),
    h<u>ea</u>rt (hahrt)

air   c<u>a</u>rry (**kair** ee), b<u>ear</u> (bair),
    wh<u>ere</u> (whair)

aw   <u>a</u>ll (awl), l<u>aw</u> (law),
    b<u>ough</u>t (bawt)

ay   s<u>ay</u> (say), br<u>ea</u>k (brayk),
    v<u>ei</u>n (vayn)

e   b<u>e</u>t (bet), s<u>ay</u>s (sez),
    d<u>ea</u>f (def)

ee   b<u>ee</u> (bee), t<u>ea</u>m (teem),
    f<u>ea</u>r (feer)

i   b<u>i</u>t (bit), w<u>o</u>men (**wim** uhn),
    b<u>ui</u>ld (bild)

I   <u>i</u>ce (is), l<u>ie</u> (lI), sk<u>y</u> (skI)

o   h<u>o</u>t (hot), w<u>a</u>tch (wotch)

oh   <u>o</u>pen (**oh** puhn), s<u>ew</u> (soh)

oi   b<u>oi</u>l (boil), b<u>oy</u> (boi)

oo   p<u>oo</u>l (pool), m<u>o</u>ve (moov),
    sh<u>oe</u> (shoo)

or   <u>or</u>der (**or** dur), m<u>ore</u> (mor)

ou   h<u>ou</u>se (hous), n<u>ow</u> (nou)

u   g<u>oo</u>d (gud), sh<u>ou</u>ld (shud)

uh   c<u>u</u>p (kuhp), fl<u>oo</u>d (fluhd),
    b<u>u</u>tt<u>o</u>n (**buht** uhn)

ur   b<u>ur</u>n (burn), p<u>ear</u>l (purl),
    b<u>ir</u>d (burd)

yoo   <u>u</u>se (yooz), f<u>ew</u> (fyoo),
    v<u>iew</u> (vyoo)

hw   <u>wh</u>at (hwuht), <u>wh</u>en (hwen)

TH   <u>th</u>at (THat), brea<u>the</u> (breeTH)

zh   mea<u>s</u>ure (**mezh** ur),
    gara<u>ge</u> (guh **razh**)

abuse of power: the use of a powerful position to do something illegal or improper

accusation (ak yoo **zay** shuhn): claim that someone has done something wrong

activist: someone who works to produce political or social change

agency (**ay** juhn see): office or business that provides services to the public

ally (**al** ı): person or country that gives support to another

ancestry (**an** ses tree): a person's relatives, going back far in the past

assembly: one house of the state legislature

barrack (**ber** uhk): building or buildings where soldiers live

base: a center that supports a military operation, including training people for military duties

bill: a written proposal for a new law, to be discussed and voted on by lawmakers

biodiversity (bı oh duh **vur** suh tee): when a wide variety of plants and animals live in a single area

cabinet: a group of people who advise the head of state, such as the president

campaign (kam **payn**): a period of time before an election when candidates try to get people to vote for them

ceremony (**ser** uh moh nee): a formal event held to celebrate an important occasion, such as a wedding, graduation, or presidential inauguration

challah (kah luh *or* **hah** luh): a rich, eggy bread, usually braided, that is often served on the Jewish Sabbath or holidays

chlorofluorocarbons (CFCs) (klawr oh flawr oh **kahr** buhnz): a type of chemical compound, created by use of air conditioners and some spray cans, that floats up into the air and causes the ozone layer to thin

civilian (si **vil** yuhn): someone who is not in armed forces such as the army, navy, or air force

civil rights: the rights that all members of a society have to freedom and equal treatment under the law

Clean Air Act: a United States law to protect the air from pollution; first passed in 1967 as the Air Quality Act and amended in 1970 as the Clean Air Act

Clean Water Act: a United States law passed in 1972 to protect lakes, streams, and oceans from pollution

commissioner (kuh **mish** uh nur): a person in charge of solving a particular problem or doing certain tasks

Communist (kom yoo nist): person who supports a system of government in which businesses and property are controlled by the state

company: a unit of soldiers

conscience (kon shuhns): an inner feeling of what is right and what is wrong

conservation (kon sur **vay** shuhn): protection of valuable things such as forests, wildlife, and natural resources from change, loss, or damage

conserve: to save something from loss or decay

counselor: someone who gives advice

court of appeals: the second level in the federal judicial system, also known as circuit court

crisis (**krı** sis): a time of danger and difficulty, or a turning point

debate (duh **bayt**): to discuss between sides with different points of view

decency (**dee** suhn see): thoughtful, kind, or respectable behavior

democracy (di **mok** ruh see): a way of governing a country in which the people choose their own leaders in elections

Democratic Party: one of the 2 main political parties of the United States

demonstrating: gathering with others in public to display feelings for or against something

developer (di **vel** uh pur): person who plans and builds buildings and communities

dictator: someone who has complete control of a country, often ruling it unjustly

disband: to break up as a group or organization

discrimination (dis krim uh **nay** shuhn): unfair treatment of people based on differences such as race, age, gender, or place of birth

disloyal: not faithful to one's country, family, friends, or beliefs

distinguish (dis **ting** gwish): mark someone or something as separate or different from others

district court: the lowest level trial court in the judicial system

Earth Day: a day first set aside on April 22, 1970, to call attention to the environment

easygoing: relaxed

ecosystem (**ee** koh sis tuhm): a community of animals and plants that depend on each other and their environment

endangered: in danger of disappearing

environment (en **vi** ruhn muhnt): the natural world of land, sea, and air in which people, animals, and plants live

environmentalist: someone who works to protect the natural world

Environmental Protection Agency (**EPA**): a government organization formed in 1970 to enforce the laws protecting the environment

equal rights: the same rights given to all people, regardless of their race, gender, or age

flourish (**flur** ish): grow and succeed

ghetto (**get** oh): a usually poor city neighborhood where people of the same race, religion, or ethnic background live, often not by choice

girds (gurdz): prepares for a difficult job

global: something that relates to the whole world

global warming: an apparent, gradual rise in the temperature of the Earth's atmosphere, caused by the greenhouse effect

governor's mansion: a special home owned by the state where its governor lives

Great Depression: an event during the 1930s, when many people lost their jobs and homes, and people all over the United States and other countries suffered

habitat: the place or environment where a plant or animal naturally or normally lives

heifer (**hef** ur): a young cow that has never had a calf

Adolf Hitler (**ay** dolf **hit** lur): a dictator who ruled Germany from 1933 to 1945

imprint: a strong influence or lasting effect on someone or something

inaugurated: sworn into office with a formal ceremony

incumbent: someone currently holding an office or position

instinct: behavior that is natural rather than learned

integrate (**in** tuh grayt): to make facilities or organizations open to people of all races and ethnic groups

investigating: finding out as much as possible about something or someone

judicial (joo **dish** uhl): to do with a court of law or judge

landfill: garbage that is stacked and covered with earth

legacy (**leg** uh see): something that is handed down from one generation to another

legislator (**lej** uh slay tur): someone who writes and passes laws

legislature (**lej** uh slay chur): an elected group of people who have the power to make laws for the city, state, or nation

luxury (**luhk** shur ee): expensive and beautiful surroundings that make life comfortable and pleasant

mission (**mish** uhn): a particular task given to a person or group to carry out

modest (**mod** ist): not wanting to show off or draw attention to oneself

mutual (**myoo** choo uhl): the same feelings shared by 2 or more people or groups

National Guard: standby military units that can be called into service by federal or state governments

natural resource: a material that is part of nature, such as water, air, and plants

Nazi (**not** zee): describing the followers of Adolf Hitler, who wanted to rid Europe of Jews and other peoples they considered "impure"

network: a group of people who exchange information

Officer Candidate School: where people are trained to become officers in the military

ozone: a form of oxygen that sits between the sun and Earth to protect the Earth from the sun's harmful rays

penalty (**pen** uhl tee): punishment

pesticide: a chemical used to kill pests, such as insects

phosphate (**fahs** fayt): a type of chemical

political: having to do with the way a city, state, or nation governs itself

politics: the way a city, state, or nation governs itself

pollution (puh **loo** shuhn): something that dirties or destroys the natural environment

preserve: protect something so that it stays in its original state

Presidential (prez uh **den** shuhl) **Medal of Freedom**: an award given to someone who has served the country in an outstanding way

progressive: in favor of positive change

racial integration (**ray** shuhl in tuh **gray** shuhn): the end of the practice of keeping groups apart based on the color of their skin

recreational (rek ree **ay** shuh nuhl): done or used for pleasure or relaxation

recreation (rek ree **ay** shun) **area**: place where activities are meant to be enjoyed, like sports or games or fishing or swimming

recruited (ree **kroo** tid): called upon to serve in the military or to be part of a group or cause

Red Cross: a worldwide organization that helps victims of disasters such as earthquakes, floods, and war

renewable energy: power from sources that can never be used up, such as wind, waves, and the sun

Republican Party: one of the 2 main political parties in the United States

second lieutenant (loo **ten** uhnt): an entry-level officer in the United States military

segregated: separated for the purpose of keeping groups apart based on the color of their skin

Senate: in the federal government, the house of Congress where states are represented equally. In state government, districts are represented equally in the Senate.

senator: a member of the Senate, which is one house of state or federal legislature

steward (**stoo** urd): person who assists or cares for something

sustainable: lasting for long periods of time

teach-in: a meeting held to teach a group of people about a particular issue

toxin (**tok** suhn): any material that is harmful or poisonous

unanimously (yoo **nan** i muhs lee): with everyone's agreement

United States representative: person elected to Congress to speak or act for a particular region

whistle-stop: a railroad station where someone running for political office would make speeches to the people of the town

women's suffrage (**wim** uhnz **suhf** rij): the right for women to vote in elections, earned in 1920

wordsmith: someone who uses words well

Works Progress Administration (ad min uh **stray** shuhn) **(WPA)**: a national program of projects such as building roads and bridges; designed to accomplish needed tasks as well as to put people back to work during the Great Depression

Youth Conservation Corps (cor): a national program that put young people to work on projects that helped to keep our natural resources healthy, including planting trees and working in parks

Reading Group Guide and Activities

Discussion Questions

❖ More than once, Gaylord Nelson argued an unpopular position. Give 3 examples of times that he took a stand and discuss whether you agree with his actions. Then describe a time when you took an unpopular position. What was the outcome? How did you feel about it?

❖ Describe how Gaylord Nelson's ideas have changed the way people have behaved in order to stop harming the environment since the first Earth Day. Interview a parent or teacher about what changes they have seen in their lifetimes as people learned more about the environment. Have you or your family changed your own lifestyles? What other kinds of things could you do?

❖ Gaylord faced many disappointments in his life. Give 3 examples of such disappointments and how he dealt with them. What can you learn from Gaylord? Name some disappointments you have faced in your life. How did you deal with them? Describe the way you feel about them now.

❖ Explain how Gaylord's parents' involvement in the politics of their neighborhood, their larger community, and state government affected his life and career. In what ways did his activism reflect their interests? In what ways did he strike out on his own? If you could become an activist, what cause would you champion? Explain what you would want to see changed.

Activities

❧ Some plants and animals may become extinct if we don't take care to save their habitats. That's why their names appear on a list of endangered species. On the website of the Wisconsin Department of Natural Resources, http://www.dnr.state.wi.us/org/land/er/, you can see what the endangered resources are in our state. If you don't live in Wisconsin, find out the endangered resources of your state. Find 3 plants or animals that are endangered and explain why each is in trouble and what's being done to help.

❧ Look at the letter that appeared in *What Are Me and You Gonna Do?* Would it persuade you to work with the writer? Why or why not? Think of a neighborhood, local, or state issue that you would like someone in government to address. Find the people to whom you should write, and write your own letter, explaining the way Gaylord Nelson's example has affected what you have chosen to do.

❧ Create a chart, poster, or cartoon to demonstrate the way people's actions affect the environment around them. Use it in an Earth Day celebration.

❧ Imagine you have been elected to improve your school's environmental performance. Create a chart with 2 columns. In the column on the left, identify 3 school practices that you would like to see changed. In the column on the right, make specific suggestions to improve each area.

❧ List the things that you would like to see done if you were to organize a cleanup day or a tree planting for your school in honor of Earth Day.

Activities from the Earth Day Network

❧ Organize a cleanup day or a tree planting for your school.

❧ Create an environmental mascot for your school. Have a contest to see who comes up with the best mascot and slogan.

❧ Have a contest to monitor the amount of trash each class creates after lunch (the same can be done with recycling). Keep a graph for one week to see which class disposes the least amount of trash (or recycles the most) overall.

To Learn More about Earth Day and Gaylord Nelson

Books

Gardner, Robert. *Celebrating Earth Day: A Source Book of Activities and Experiments*. Minneapolis: Millbrook Press, 1992.

Lowery, Linda. *Earth Day*. Minneapolis: Carolrhoda Books, Inc., 1991.

Nelson, Gaylord. *What Are Me and You Gonna Do?* New York: Ballantine Books, 1971.

Rogers, Teresa, and Jeffrey Shulman. *Gaylord Nelson: A Day for the Earth*. Minneapolis: Twenty-First Century Books/Henry Holt, 1992.

Schwartz, Linda. *Earth Book for Kids: Activities to Help Heal the Environment*. Grand Junction, CO: Learning Works, 1990.

Newspapers and Other Materials

Earth Day Network: www.earthday.net

The Wilderness Society: www.wilderness.org

Wisconsin State Historical Society Archives: www.wisconsinhistory.org

Wisconsin State Journal and *Capital Times* archives: www.madison.com/archives/

DVDs

Earth Day and Beyond: Gaylord Nelson's Good Fight. Green Bay, WI: Newist/CESA7, 2005.

Gaylord Nelson: A Profile. Madison: Wisconsin Educational Communications Board, 2005.

Acknowledgments

It was a pleasure to research and write about a person as extraordinary as Gaylord Nelson. His determination to leave the Earth a better place and his courage to take action were inspirational to me. Because of him, the young people who read this book are living in a cleaner, safer environment than their grandparents grew up in.

I am grateful to the many sources of information that helped me to make this a factual account of Nelson's many contributions. But above all, I wish to thank the Nelson family for helping to make this notable historical figure come alive. It was an honor to interview Gaylord's wife, Carrie Lee Nelson, and all of his adult children, Gaylord Jr., Tia, and Jeff, who generously shared their time and memories with me.

Much appreciation goes out to Charles Clark, a Clear Lake resident and friend of the Nelson family. A visit with him in Gaylord's hometown included a tour of Gaylord's boyhood haunts and the museum that Clark founded to commemorate Gaylord's life. Each stop, complete with firsthand stories about Gaylord's childhood, helped me to understand why Clear Lake was such an important pillar in Gaylord Nelson's life.

In addition, Karen Ohm, a teacher at the Gaylord A. Nelson Educational Center in Clear Lake, took time out of her busy day to show me examples of how Earth Day has been celebrated at the elementary school that Gaylord periodically visited. Thanks too to Nancy Piraino, science teacher at Madison Memorial High School, who offered helpful suggestions for classroom activities.

Photos contributed by Tia Nelson; Charles Clark; Marcus Cohen; the Wisconsin Historical Society; Eric Sherman, director of the Ice Age Park and Trail Foundation; and Dennis McCormick, librarian at the Capital Newspapers archives in Madison, were invaluable additions in lending a visual account of Gaylord's life. Thank you to Elizabeth Boone, John Nondorf, and Kate Carey for their expertise in artfully using the photos to help tell the tale.

And, of course, no book would be complete without the careful scrutiny of a fine editor, which I had in Michelle Wildgen of the Wisconsin Historical Society Press. Michelle left no stone unturned in our mutual quest to make this an authentic picture of a great man.

Bobbie Malone, director of the Office of School Services for the Wisconsin State Historical Society, was instrumental in bringing this book to fruition by recognizing the value of adding Gaylord Nelson's name to the list of Badger Biographies. Her insightful knowledge of how to transform history into readable content for children was invaluable.

They say it takes a village. I had an excellent one. Thank you to each and every person who graciously contributed to this project.

Index

This index points you to the pages where you can read about persons, places, and ideas. If you do not find the word you are looking for, try to think of another word that means about the same thing.

When you see a page number in **bold** it means there is a picture on that page.